THANK YOU SAMMY

Brian R. King, LCSW
Illustrations By: Ray Gulzeth

THANK YOU SAMMY

Brian R. King, LCSW

Illustrations by Ray Gulzeth

© Brian R. King 2008

Published by 1stWorld Publishing
P.O. Box 2211, Fairfield, Iowa 52556
tel: 641-209-5000 • fax: 866-440 5234
web: www.1stworldpublishing.com

First Edition

LCCN: 2008935233

ISBN: 978-1-4218-9025-8
eBook ISBN: 978-1-4218-9026-5

All rights reserved. No part of this book may be reproduced or utilized in any form or by any means, electronic or mechanical, including photocopying or recording, or by any information storage and retrieval system, without permission in writing from the author.

This material has been written and published solely for educational purposes. The author and the publisher shall have neither liability nor responsibility to any person or entity with respect to any loss, damage or injury caused or alleged to be caused directly or indirectly by the information contained in this book.

The sun's starting to come up over the top of the forest trees, and the dew covering the leaves is glistening from the light. One by one the forest animals begin lifting their heads. Each creature lets out a big yawn, and then takes a big stretch in preparation for the new day. Though most everyone is just beginning to wake, our friend Sammy Squirrel has been up and about for many hours now. He has so much energy that he just jumps out of bed and gets to work.

Sammy lives in the hollow part of the Granddaddy Oak Tree, the biggest tree in the whole forest. First thing every morning he climbs to the top and looks out across all of the land to make sure everything is okay and things are just as he left them.

After that he finds the branch with the wettest leaves and gently climbs onto it. Then he jumps up and down so all of the water pours over him, giving him a nice cool shower. When he's all clean, he picks a fresh berry and squeezes a few drops of juice on his head then eats the berry. He thinks the juice makes him smell sweet and his breath smell like candy.

After Sammy finishes his shower, it's time for breakfast. This morning he has a special craving for those chewy nuts that grow on the other end of the forest. So he takes a running leap off the end of the branch and spreads his wings wide. Sammy is a flying squirrel, so he just glides through the air and lands firmly on the branch of another tree. Then he hops from tree to tree until he gets to the one he is looking for. He lands on a small limb that begins to bend under his weight. He quickly wraps his legs around it as tight as he can so he won't fall off. Sammy waits until the branch stops bending; then digs his claws into it and runs to the bottom. He reaches the base of the branch where he finds the most delicious looking nut he has ever seen.

Just as he begins to reach for it, he hears a - SNAP! SNAP! - Coming from the ground below. It's the sound of breaking twigs. "Oh Hi Danny," he says, seeing his friend Danny Deer walking down below.

"Good Morning Sammy," Danny replies looking up.

"It certainly is. Whatcha doin' Dan?"

"I'm really hungry Sammy," he says with a sigh.

"Why don't yah eat somethin' then?"

"There's nothing to eat!" I've been walking around the forest for three days now, and all of the bushes are either dried up or have no berries left."

"Don't worry Danny, you just haven't been looking in the right places. Just follow me." Sammy begins to hop back across the tops of the trees, but is sure to go slow enough that the tired and hungry Danny Deer can keep up.

Soon they arrive back at the Grand-daddy Oak. "Are we there yet?" a weary Danny asks.

"Look up," Sammy replies excitedly. "Granddaddy Oak has tons of berries ripe for the picking, and they sure are sweet."

"I didn't know Oak trees have berries," said a surprised Danny.

"This is a very special Oak Tree," replied Sammy.

"Wow!" Danny says amazed, "but I can't eat those berries Sammy, they belong to you."

"No they don't," he states emphatically, "they belong to the Granddaddy oak, I just live here. These berries are for everyone." Then Sammy bites off the stems of five big clumps of berries, and each one falls to the ground where Danny can eat them.

Sammy scurries down the trunk of the tree and looks on as Danny eats the berries to fill his hungry stomach. "Those are good, huh Danny; just like I said."

Danny's mouth curls with a big smile. "Thank you Sammy. You really did me a favor, I owe you one."

"It wasn't a favor," Sammy replies, "I just did what needed to be done. You were hungry and needed some food. I knew where some was so I took you there. That's all."

"But you didn't have to help me Sammy. That's why I owe you one."

"Okay, if you think so then all you have to do is help someone like I helped you. How's that sound?"

"It sounds great Sammy. Thanks again, I'll see you later," Danny states as he prances back into the forest.

Sammy runs back up to the top of the oak tree where he left the nuts he'd brought back with him. He carries them inside his hole and has a nice breakfast. He eats them with a smile, happy that he was able to help Danny.

After breakfast, Sammy grabs his homemade pinecone toothbrush and brushes his teeth until they are sparkling clean. Then he goes to stand in the doorway of his home to enjoy the fresh morning breeze.

He looks down and sees his good friend Rita Rabbit. She's up early this morning too so she can collect water for her carrot patch. As he watches he notices that Rita is limping, which makes her spill her water with every step. He knows she needs help so he quickly climbs down the tree. "Wait a second Rita, let me help." He takes the water filled acorn cap from her paw, and carries it the rest of the way. He sits the cap down next to the carrot patch so he and Rita can talk.

"What's wrong with your foot Rita?" Sammy asks, concerned.

"Well Sammy. I stepped on a big thorn the other day, and now my foot is so swollen I can barely walk."

"It sounds like you need to rest that foot."

"I know I do," Rita replies, "but my carrots need to be watered every day. If they aren't they might die, and then I won't have any food to eat."

"Don't worry Rita You can go back to your burrow and rest your foot, and I'll water your carrots."

"You will Sammy!" She exclaims. "But won't that be a lot of trouble?"

"Not at all. It won't take me long to water your carrots. You rest now Rita, and don't worry, your carrots will be taken care of."

"Oh thank you Sammy, I don't know how I'll ever repay you."

"That's all right, when your foot is healed and you can walk comfortably again, then I will enjoy watching you tend your carrot patch That is enough thanks for me." Sammy takes her by the paw and helps her back to her burrow.

"Thank you Sammy," she says.

Sammy hurries down to the stream and fills Rita's acorn cap with water. He has just enough water for every carrot in the patch. He Finishes his chore quickly then walks back home to take a nap; it has been a busy morning.

As the forest turns from day into night a huge thunderstorm rolls in. A strong wind blows through the Granddaddy Oak tree. Then CRASH goes the lightning. BOOOM, rolls the thunder. The rain begins pouring down.

While Sammy sleeps, some of the rain starts to leak into his hole. Then a small drop falls and hits Sammy on the head. Startled, he sits up in bed. "What was that?" he exclaims, before realizing how hard it is raining. He walks over to the doorway. Gazing down he can't believe his eyes. "Oh my goodness! Rita's carrots are being washed away by the rain!"

The rain is coming so fast that the forest begins to flood. The water is so high that Sammy has to swim through its cold depth to get to the carrot patch. He paddles as hard and as fast as he can to get there before all is lost. As the water moves swiftly through the garden, some of the carrots come out of the ground and begin floating toward the river. Using his teeth and paws, he grabs as many of them as he can. Then he swims over to a rock nearby and sticks the carrots underneath it where they will be safe and won't float away. Sammy spends an hour swimming back and forth in the cold water. Luckily he is able to save all of Rita's carrots. Now she won't have to go hungry.

Little does Sammy know, that off in the the distance Rita, having been forced out of her flooded burrow is watching him brave the storm to protect her food. She is so grateful for what Sammy did, that a tear runs down her cheek.

As Rita continues to look on, Sammy swims back to his tree and slowly climbs back into his hole. "Aaaaaaaah Choo!" Sammy lets out a big sneeze. "Oh doh," he says with a sniffle. "I tink I hab a cold." Then he climbs into his nice warm bed.

Two days pass and Rita waits patiently for Sammy to come outside so she can thank him for all he had done. Her foot is all better now so she is out working in her carrot patch, putting all of the carrots back into the ground so they can finish growing. A moment later Danny Deer appears through the brush.

"Hi Rita. How are you today?"

"Very well thanks. By the way where's Sammy? I haven't seen him in two days."

"I don't know Rita. I'm just coming to visit him myself." Danny goes on to tell her all about how Sammy had helped him when he was hungry. He has come because he found a big delicious berry bush just outside the forest, and brought some of its berries for Sammy to eat. He wants to thank Sammy again for his help.

Then Rita tells Danny about her sore foot, and all the things Sammy had done for her. Especially how he had heroically braved the storm to rescue her carrots. He's such a wonderful friend," says Rita, "we should do something for him."

"Yes we should," replies Danny with his head held high. But where is he?"

"AAAAAAAAH CHOOOOO!" They hear a sound from above.

"Did Granddaddy Oak just sneeze?" asks Danny.

"AH CHOO AH CHOO!" They heard it again.

"That came from Sammy's hole," Rita says.

"Yeah," Danny exclaims, "I'll bet he has a cold after being out in that storm the other night."

"That's it," Rita shouts "I know just what we'll do for Sammy to pay him back." They begin preparing, and by the next morning they are ready. Danny is the only one tall enough to reach Sammy's hole.

He leans over and sets his head on the ground. Rita grabs the package they prepared and climbs onto Danny's head. Then Danny walks over to the Granddaddy Oak and stands up on his hind legs so he can look right into Sammy's hole. "HI SAMMY!" They say as Rita steps down from Danny's head and into Sammy's hole. Sammy sits up with a look of surprise. "Hi guys."

"Don't get up Sammy, you lie back down and rest." Danny says.

"I hab a bad cold."

"We know," Rita replies, "that's why we're here."

"What do you mean?" Sammy asks.

"When we needed help, you took care of us," Danny explains, "So we are here to take care of you."

Rita opens up the package and pulls out a piping hot bowl of carrot soup. She sets it down next to Sammy's bed. "I made this from the carrots in my patch, the carrots that you saved from the storm. Thank you Sammy," Rita says. "Now you drink every drop of this soup, and it will make you feel better."

She reaches back into the package and pulls out a big, fluffy blanket and drapes it over him. "Here Sammy. I shed my fur all the time and I know how warm it keeps me, so I took a bunch of it and knitted this blanket so that it can keep you warm too."

"Thanks Rita," he says with a smile. "I feel better already."

"Here Sammy," says Danny. "I brought you some fresh berries to eat. I also found some of those chewy nuts you like so much. They're full of vitamins so they should help you get better."

"Thanks Dan, thanks a lot. What would I do without you guys?"
"Without us you might have gone hungry," Danny explains, "like we would have if it hadn't been for you. You see Sammy, friends help each other, so now we're helping you."

"You helped us out of the kindness of your heart Sammy," Rita continues. "And for no other reason. You've taught Danny and me what real friendship is all about. And we love you for all you've done."

"Thanks guys," Sammy sighs, "but I just did what needed doing. I see something that doesn't look right and I want to fix it. If something seems out of place I want to put it back in place. That's what I do guys, I was only being myself"

"You're right Sammy" said Danny. You always seem to know where everything is in the forest, almost like you have a picture of it in your head"

Rita continued, "You're always on the lookout for everyone and everything in this forest to make sure that everything is as it should be and all of us are okay."

"Well the forest is my home" Sammy explained. "If something is wrong in my home then I'm not happy. I guess I did't realize that by doing what makes sense to me to do was actually helping other folks too."

Rita then placed her paw on Sammy's head and said, "Sammy. No matter why you do the things you do, you are very special through and through. So you just keep on being that special you because making yourself happy makes us happy too."

Sammy got a tear in his eye and said, "I never realized that just being myself could mean so much. I've always just been myself and nothing more."

Then Danny and Rita said together," And that's why we love you. Thank you Sammy."

About The Author

Brian R. King is a Licensed Clinical Social Worker in private practice in which he brings a unique three fold perspective to the world of Asperger's. Brian not only has two sons on the Autism Spectrum and a practice focusing exclusively on working with Asperger's clients and their families. Brian is also blessed with Asperger's himself.

Brian has become known worldwide for his positive approach to Living the Asperger's experience and is dedicating his time to serving as an Ambassador between the Asperger and Neurotypical communities. His goal is to help both communities learn to better communicate, appreciate and cooperate with each other in a spirit of mutual respect. You can learn more about Brian at www.ImAnAspie.com

See 1stWorld Books at:

www.1stWorldPublishing.com

See our classic collection at:

www.1stWorldLibrary.com

A bald eagle is also seen along the way.

Once again the dolphins swim about and play beside the boat. Then, Mommy asked if the girls enjoyed their boat cruise. Alexia said "Yes." Sofia asked if they could all go out on Double Sunshine again another day.

Mommy and Daddy smile! It was a wonderful family outing and the girls are happy to have enjoyed watching for dolphins, birds and other wildlife!

Sophia says, "Thank you for the boat cruise" to Double Sunshine's Captain Dan. Both Alexia and Sophia say "Goodbye" to him.

Then, Alexia says; "I wonder what will happen the next time we all go out on Double Sunshine?"

The girls will surely tell all their friends and family members about the wonderful boat cruise they had after leaving the dock at Tin City!

Photo Gallery

Bald Eagle

Dolphin

Egret

Osprey

Pelican

www.ingramcontent.com/pod-product-compliance
Lightning Source LLC
Chambersburg PA
CBHW041537040426
42446CB00002B/121